Matt Bacak's

Discover a proven, but little-known system to tap into your niche market, bring in more leads, sell more products and explode your internet sales

The Ultimate Lead Generation Plan

The Ultimate Lead Generation Plan

By Matt Bacak

ISBN: 1-933596-48-1 (Paperback)

ISBN: 1-933596-64-3 (eBook)

Published by:

MORGAN · JAMES

THE ENTREPRENEURIAL PUBLISHER

Morgan James Publishing, LLC

1225 Franklin Ave Ste 325

Garden City, NY 11530-1693

Toll Free 800-485-4943

www.MorganJamesPublishing.com

Habitat for Humanity®
Peninsula
Building Partner

Interior Design by:

Heather Kirk

www.GraphicsByHeather.com

Heather@GraphicsByHeather.com

Acknowledgements

I first would like to say thank You, Lord, who in all things are possible! You have blessed me indeed! I would like to thank my beautiful wife for standing behind me through thick and thin. And for all the sacrifices we have made together. To my daughters — Taylor, I love you with all my heart, and to our new wee one on her way, Daddy can't wait until you're in his arms!

To my mom and dad, for all their support and encouragement through the years. My brother, thanks for everything you have done, thanks for being you! I look up to you. My grandparents, thank you so much. My incredible team, Erick, Tera, Josh, Craig, Devon and Sara, thank you. To all my loyal subscribers and clients, without all, this book would never be possible! To my wife's parents for letting me take her away.

To the people that I do not speak of for all the things you taught me not to do. To my fraternity brother, IN HOC! To my aunts and uncles, to my cousins. Thank you to my friends online and offline, thanks for your support. Thanks to my book team: Warren; David, my publisher; Heather, my graphics.

And to you, the reader of this book, thank you so much for your support! May you find some gems in this book that put money into your pocket, through the leads you generate.

Reader, what I always tell my friends and now you...This is just the beginning. Everyday is just the beginning. May God bless you, and may you take action implementing these powerful strategies. I truly care about your results. I have been in your shoes — I can help you. Please let me try!

Warmest regards,

Matt Bacak

Foreword

The million-dollar skill in business is learning how to generate quality leads for your business. Unfortunately, we all hear stories of a motivated individuals starting a business, getting all excited, and then six months down the road, they ask, "How do I generate leads, how do I get clients?"

The lack of knowledge and training in this area destroys so many entrepreneurial lives.

Here's some good news though.

You are holding in your hands a book that could dramatically change your business life.

You're about to start learning proven tactics that you could immediately start applying in your business which could quickly start to raise your income.

Also, what's exciting about discovering these secrets is you'll be able to make more money, working fewer hours.

Matt Bacak has helped thousands of businesses increase their income by using his proven strategies.

He's a true expert because he 'walks his talk' and his personal results speak for themselves.

After reading *The Ultimate Lead Generation Plan*, I was planning on writing a three or four page foreword telling you about some parts you really need to read carefully, but I decided against it.

Why?

Because I don't want you to waste anytime and you need to quickly jump inside *The Ultimate Lead Generation Plan* and start using these secrets to million dollar lead generation because it will change your life.

Start right now!

You are about to embark on a great journey, enjoy it!

Mike Litman

#1 Best-Selling Author of
Conversations with Millionaires
www.MikeLitman.com

The Ultimate Lead Generation Plan
For $327 In FREE Bonuses Go To: www.PromotingTips.com/3Bonuses.htm

Table Of Contents

Introduction

*T*his information is going to blow your mind...

If you want to learn how to sell more product...

If you want to drive tons of traffic to your websites...

*If you want to **really explode** your online newsletter, ezine or e-course opt-Ins...*

If you want to know how to get more butts in seminar seats...

If you want to make more cold hard cash...

Then you need to start building that database now!

You need to start collecting names and you've got to do it the right way. We truly want to help you become successful or become more successful than you already are and we are all about giving you the techniques, the tips, the tools, the information that you need to create that success.

I appreciate the opportunity to share with you the following pages, it's really an honor. There are tons of amazing things we're doing on the Internet and we are going to dive into it.

How can you generate leads?

I'm going to share with you step-by-step my *Ultimate Lead Generation Plan*. It's so powerful that I call it the Lead Explosion System. And I'm going to share it with you. You may want to grab your highlighter to mark important information or a pen and your notebook to write down the ideas you create while reading. I'm going to tell you step-by-step how to do things. But not only that, I'm going to show you as much as I can in this book, my business model.

I went from flat broke. Bankrupt. I had lost everything that I had, then I was able to build it all back into a multi-million dollar business by using the information that I'm going to share with you in this book. Inside this book, I'll teach you what I would do if I lost all of my websites, my businesses and everything. Basically, I'll be answering this question: What would I do if my business vanished right now? What would be the steps that I would take?

The Ultimate Lead Generation Plan
For $327 In FREE Bonuses Go To: www.PromotingTips.com/3Bonuses.htm

Before we dive into it, I also have to tell you this — consider it a warning or take comfort in it — I'm not an author; I'm a marketer. I started as a promoter and I have been behind the scenes with tons of famous people. I did things with the Rich Dad organization — I was a Certified Facilitator for Cash Flow 101 events. I was promoting and putting on those events; promoting seminars in the real estate market; and promoting people in the self-help arena. I've been promoting a lot of people out there; I have been in tons of different markets. And I have found that it doesn't matter what kind of business you're in these strategies work for every business. You'll discover a breakthrough marketing system guaranteed to increase the profits of any online business — even yours! The same strategies that I'm going to show you in this book are the same strategies that work for a bricks and mortar business like the restaurant that I just recently bought.

So you will definitely be able to use my methods in your business — no matter what it is. This is going to be so revolutionary for your business! Just make sure you know that it doesn't matter where you're at in business, these strategies will work for you. When you finish reading you will be able to tweak the strategies to use for yourself.

Just modify them a little bit.

Most readers are in a similar situation in that they are promoting their business's product or information or someone else's products.

Matt Bacak

Chapter 1

Controlling Your Future

Chapter 1: Controlling your Future

*H*ere's why the information I'm about to tell you is so powerful. When I got started as a promoter, I was putting on seminars. And there was a strategy that I used on a regular basis to put 50 to 100 people in a seminar room in less than 3 days just by sending out a few emails.

When doing this, I discovered the power of Joint Ventures. I would go out and find people or companies that had huge mailing lists. That doesn't mean cold calling a bunch of people. I developed business relationships and friendships with them.

I gave first.

These relationships were and are so valuable because they became my joint venture partners.

Then, I'd ask them to send out emails to their lists selling my event. That way they would pass on their credibility with the list to me and their list to make my event occur. But then something happened that changed things for me.

I was promoting an event and several joint venture partners had committed to making it happen. But all of the list-owners ended-up realizing that they had another email message that they needed to send to their list at that same time.

They had another promotion. They just couldn't get my email out. They had to put their businesses first. And my event just didn't happen. That was when I realized that you have got to have your own insurance policy. What I mean by that is, it's all about having your own list.

Because, your list is your goldmine!

So the lesson is that joint ventures are an incredible way to make money and build your lists but you never have control. That leaves your destiny in the hands of other people.

As you continue reading, you will learn how to get that control. Not only, having that control, but having the power to send out emails and make money whatever you want. **The power belongs to the one who controls the list.** Some like to say that your money is in your list.

I've been behind the scenes as a promoter. That's why online they call me the Powerful Promoter because of the good ol' days I just told you about. But I'm not only a promoter, but I'm also a marketer.

I love sitting on my butt and making money. I'm going to show you how you can do the same.

Chapter 2

Can You Really Help Me

Chapter 2: Can You Really Help Me

Now a lot of people ask me, 'Matt, why are you confident to offer this Powerful Lead Explosion System?' My answer is always this, "I make money using the system and so do my clients. Thus, it is a time-tested and refined system. Further, I am confident because with my technical engineering and marketing backgrounds, I understand the tools that actually work… from a marketing perspective and from a technical perspective."

When I was in college, I graduated with a marketing degree, a BS in Marketing. At the same time, I got a technical engineering degree. I went back and forth from school to school. I ended up graduating from both schools at the same time. I got my Associates degree in Technical Engineering and my BS in Marketing. Here's the interesting thing. After getting out in the real world and applying the "stuff" they taught us (more like they regurgitated from a book), I realized that I was right all along… my marketing degree was BS. To this day I still think it's B.S.

The best thing about getting this information from me is that is I can and will tell you the things that actually do work. I will break it down and simplify it for you, because the biggest thing I see out there is a lot of people that understand either the technical side or they understand the marketing side. But they never understand both. I'm able and willing to break it down and make it so easy for you to understand. I will also pull in skills that I developed because my keen observation and the mentoring I did under some great marketing minds.

Among the great marketing minds that I have spent time with some are millionaires and some are billionaires. Yes, billionaires (Forbes report in May 2005 that there were a total of 691 in the entire world). And I got to sit around with them. Talking to them, finding out things, it was just amazing and I'm going to share with you things that I've learned from them later in the book.

Also, another question a lot of people ask me is like why should I invest my money and time with you versus the alternatives out there. My answer to them is this. This is the only total solution package. It's not just theory. You're going to see my system in these pages. You see, I created the system that I sought after for years and I'm going to share that system with you.

Another important factor is that I recommend tools that I personally use. I'm not going to tell you about the programs and tools out there that I don't use. I'm going to tell you things that I do use. Nothing drives me more nuts than when somebody says go use software product x and they've never even tried it. They are recommending a product they don't know anything about. I will only share with you things that I use.

Next, I spend two-thirds of my time marketing and only one-third of my time teaching how to market. And here's the biggest reason…

The number one reason that my program works better for you is because I truly care about your results and I want to see you successful. I love getting those emails when people say, "Wow, I implemented this and this is what happened…" That's my joy in doing this. I don't need to teach this information. I've got other businesses that are making money for me. but I know that sharing this information with you will help you grow, help you become more successful and I really care about you. I want to see you succeed, so I urge you to read this entire book.

If you are considering doing this alone, let me tell you how dangerous and expensive that is. I spent $65,000 and over 3 years figuring out the system that I am sharing with you here. If you think about it, it took me a long time. I was banging my head on the wall day after day after day. Just trying to figure it all out. Making the mistakes for you. Doing everything and investing my money in different places trying to figure this out. I have created the system that I searched for but didn't exist.

Chapter 3

The 3 Different Types Of Sites I Use

Chapter 3: The 3 Different Types Of Sites I Use

*T*here are 3 different types of websites that I use.

1. BRANDING SITE

Now the first kind of website that I use is what I call a branding site. This is a site that creates your brand. If you have a business, it brands your company. If you're an author, a speaker or an expert, it's a site that brands you.

Typically, these are the sites that your graphic designer/webmaster probably created for you.

It's just a page or series of pages where people can go to find out more detailed information about you. Maybe buy your products. Maybe learn about the services that you have. Maybe learn about the consulting that you offer. Maybe read about your background and things like that. Or for a business maybe it's about your company and how it started and so on and so forth.

There are always many different places for people to click and many different avenues to go down.

DEFINITION: BRANDING SITE ALLOWS PROSPECTS TO LEARN ABOUT YOU AND YOUR BUSINESS

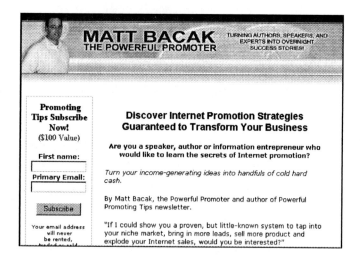

The Ultimate Lead Generation Plan
For $327 In FREE Bonuses Go To: www.PromotingTips.com/3Bonuses.htm

2. SALES LETTER SITE

The second type of website that I use is called a sales letter. If you've been around the internet world you've probably seen sales letters out there. I use sales letters all the time to sell a product or service, an event or other programs. The purpose of a sales letter is to sell your stuff.

Proprietary Method Automates Lead Generation... *So You Can Goof Off!*

"How You Can Quickly And Easily Get A Website Business System Guaranteed To Convert A Flood Of NEW, EAGER, READY Prospects... Without Spending A Fortune On Advertising, Or Hiring Expensive Experts!"

-by Matt Bacak

Build Your Business On Autopilot –This System Delivers A Predictable Number Of Leads Day After Day, Week After Week, Month After Month...

...You Only Spend Time With People Who Seek You Out, Who Already Know What You Do, And *Want To Buy* From You!

But the one we're going to talk about and spend the most time on is my favorite one to use…

DEFINITION: SALES LETTER SITE SELLS A PRODUCT, SERVICE OR EVENT

3. POWER SQUEEZE™ SITE

If you didn't highlight those other two, make sure you highlight this one! It's called a Power Squeeze™ site. What is Power Squeeze™ site? It's a site that powerfully squeezes the information you need from people. It captures their first name, their last name or whatever information you request. Whether it's for consultations or for getting people to subscribe to your reports. Whatever your offer is, the site powerfully squeezes the information from people. And there's only one outcome for the entire site.

DEFINITION: POWER SQUEEZE™ SITE CAPTURES THE CONTACT INFORMATION OF YOUR PROSPECTS

"You're About To Learn 'Secrets' That Most People Will Never Know About How To Really Explode Online Newsletter, Ezine or e-course Opt-Ins In No Time Flat..."

"If you have an email account, then you can discover *the most* powerful strategies to volcanically erupt your online newsletter opt in subscriber databases while making more cold hard cash."

— By Matt Bacak

Dear Friend,

The Powerful Promoting Tips is the one of the most real- life, here's-how-to-do-it online newsletters you'll ever find on the internet with strategies you can use to rapidly grow quality subscribers..

Discover proven, but little-known system to tap into your niche market, bring in more leads, sell more product and explode your Internet sales. For example, you'll learn strategies and secrets, like...

• **How to effectively target buyers** to your products or services;

The Ultimate Lead Generation Plan

For $327 In FREE Bonuses Go To: www.PromotingTips.com/3Bonuses.htm

If we go back and look at these 3 different types of websites, you should see three different purposes. Just like I say all the time about life, you're going to find that there are things for which there's a purpose.

I just bought a restaurant and there's a purpose for it in my life. And there's a purpose for another business that I have. And there's a purpose for me teaching others…

There's a purpose behind my having a **branding site**. The purpose I have for branding site is just to **brand me or my company**. That should be the purpose of your branding site. Again, the only outcome I look for on the branding site is to brand me or my company. It is very simple once you understand. Now I'll give you an example of one of my Branding sites and you can look this over, http://www.PowerfulPromoter.com. You can see that it provides information that allows a viewer to learn more about me and my coaching practice. I hope you are able to go review this right now so you get the full effect of what I am trying to distinguish about the site types for you.

The **sales letter site** has only one purpose — to get people to buy a specific product. I don't put tons of (or any) different products on the sales letter site. There's one outcome — to clearly focus on buying the one product that they are presented — that's it. An example of my sales letter site is http://www.LeadExplosionSystem.com. There's only one outcome on that page, to sell the free CD. Another great example of a sales letter site is my http://www.InternetMillionaireIntensive.com.

Now on the **Power Squeeze™ site** there's also only one outcome that you're looking for and that's to powerfully squeeze information out of viewers. Just getting that information necessary for you to market to them over and over and over again. A great example of my Power Squeeze™ sites is http://www.PromotingTips.com. Another favorite Power Squeeze™ that I've put up is http://www.FrontierPowerHosting.com, of course, that's for another business.

In my coaching programs, students learn to easily develop these sites for themselves. As we go deeper into this information, you'll understand why I do this. And why you should too!

Now here's an interesting thing about the Power Squeeze™ pages. If I had to start all over again, the only site that I would ever put up is a Power

The Ultimate Lead Generation Plan

Squeeze™ site, because that allows me to capture people's information and market to them over and over and over again. Now if you go back and look at a branding site, you'll realize that a lot of people put those up.

From a sales perspective, realize that a confused mind never buys. Well, when a prospect goes to a branding site and there are tons of little different things to click on, the prospect is going to click away and he or she is never going to reach the outcome that you want them to reach. That's why we have specific sites.

Now here's the important thing about Power Squeeze™ sites and the reason that I put it in the order that I did. (The order was Branding site, Sales letter site and then Power Squeeze™ sites.) Because I started noticing quite recently that either a lot of people are listening to what I have to say; or a lot of people are realizing that I'm right; or a lot of people just figured it out on their own. But they're putting their Power Squeeze™ sites in front of their Branding sites. And they're putting it in front of their sales letter sites to capture people's information.

Have you seen a site where you submit your name and email just to get to the

Chapter 3: The 3 Different Types Of Sites

information you wanted? That's a perfect example of a Power Squeeze™ leading to the Branding or Sales Letter site.

Here's the interesting thing, if you put a Power Squeeze™ site in front of one of your sales letter pages, you will find what we have tested — your conversion rate does not change.

The only thing that is changing is you are capturing more people's information, so now you have the ability to market to people more and more. It's just huge for us and it's going to be huge for you too.

Chapter 4

Destroying
Big Myths

Chapter 4: Destroying Big Myths

N ow there is a myth out there that I want to break for you right now. So fully absorb this! The myth is that you can only have one website. I run into people all the time, they say, 'Oh, I got this website, my graphic designer to put it up.' Or 'My webmaster told me to put this one up.' So they think they cannot have another website in addition to their Branding site. The truth and the fact of the matter is, it's perfectly all right to have more than one website. It's more than all right to do that. Now, I'm giving you permission to go out and put up more. Also notice the people that have more than one website, and you will start noticing that they actually have a bigger bank account as well.

Before we can start moving forward, there's another big myth out there that I need to break you free of too. That is that a lot of people believe that they need a product or service before they start building their list. People will say things like 'I don't have my own product' or 'my service isn't ready,' but they do know what kind of market they are going to get into. Yet, they think they can't start building a list until those products and services are on the shelf waiting.

Now if you are in that position, let me tell you something. Something I've learned from experience but first learned in a conversation with a multi-millionaire. This is a key element that propelled me so quickly to be in his position. Now, I have the privilege to have moved to his seat in the conversation and I can tell you with authority, "If you want to make a decent income, then go out and sell products and services. But, (here's the kicker) if you want to become insanely rich, what you want to do is create and control markets." That's what we're going to be diving into next...

The Ultimate Lead Generation Plan
For $327 In FREE Bonuses Go To: www.PromotingTips.com/3Bonuses.htm

Chapter 5

How To Create And Control Markets

Chapter 5: How To Create And Control Markets

What does it mean to create and control markets? I'm talking about building your list, building your newsletter and building your e-zines. I am talking about you having the ability to send out emails that make huge things happen for you.

You can. Quite recently, I went out and I bought a new Mercedes. I looked around, test-drove and then we were sitting there ready to buy it. My wife looked at me and said, "Okay, I've never paid this much money for a car." I said, "Well, it's fine, don't worry about it, just wait." And the next day I did a promotion and paid back the account balance because of the power of my list.

I can do this because I had the ability to send out an email to create money on demand for myself.

You will too when you listen and implement the information that I share with you.

Now here is the part that I want to really get across to you. If my business vanished right now, if I lost everything I had again. If I had to start all over, what would I do first?

IMPORTANT: READ EVERY WORD AND GRAB YOUR HIGHLIGHTER IF YOU NEED TO...

The first thing that I would do is go to a location on the Internet called <u>GoDaddy.com</u> and I would buy a domain. A domain is a web address or a URL. It's going to be less than $10 to buy a domain. First buy a domain name. When you go to <u>GoDaddy.com</u> to buy your domain make sure you only buy a domain and nothing else! (They will try to upsell you 100s of times.) The next thing I would do is go out and get a hosting account. I've tested out really expensive hosting accounts and really cheap hosting accounts and the best way to go is a private hosting account from <u>http://www.FrontierPowerHosting.com</u>. To speed things up, you can buy a domain as you set-up your hosting account with them.

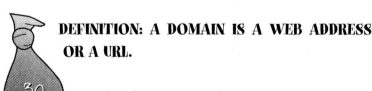

DEFINITION: A DOMAIN IS A WEB ADDRESS OR A URL.

30

The Ultimate Lead Generation Plan

For $327 In FREE Bonuses Go To: www.PromotingTips.com/3Bonuses.htm

> **ACTION STEPS:**
>
> **1.) Buy a domain name**
>
> **2.) Apply for a private hosting account with**
> **http://www.FrontierPowerHosting.com**

So the first thing I would do is buy a domain name. Go to <u>GoDaddy.com</u> and purchase it or purchase it through Frontier Power Hosting while creating your account. After you buy the domain name, then you have to have the place where you're going to start building your **empire**, where you're going to start building your web page. That is your hosting account.

Now here are a couple of significant things about this hosting provider. They provide the service for only $97 a month. And here's the unbelievably-great-deal part of <u>http://www.FrontierPowerHosting.com</u>, when you go there, not only do you get half a Gig (500MB) of hard drive space (space to house your sites on), also you have the ability to create an unlimited amount of emails. Not only an unlimited amount of emails, but an unlimited number of sites and unlimited subdomains you can add on the one account! You can go back to GoDaddy and buy another domain, and buy another domain, and buy another domain then add it to your account. In addition there are so many pieces of software included in your account — you have to see their site to believe it!

They also include ARP3 and move your current web site as part of their package with a small set-up fee of $100.

DEFINITION: HARD DRIVE SPACE IS WHERE YOU STORE ALL OF YOUR HOSTING FILES SUCH AS THE WEB SITES YOU CREATE

DEFINITION: SUBDOMAIN IS LIKE A MINI-SITE ON YOUR HOSTING ACCOUNT AND CAN BE POINTED TO DIFFERENT FOLDERS IN YOUR WEB SPACE, FOR EXAMPLE http://subdomain.mymaindomain.com

---

ACTION STEPS: You can buy as many domain names as you need. Example, for your branding site, sales letter site, Power Squeeze™ pages and etc.

When I first started, I set-up 26 websites on one account of their private hosting accounts and the price was still just $97.00 a month. I have found that most hosting companies charge a set-up fee and/or an additional monthly charge to add more domains to your hosting account so this is huge. You are only paying your annual domain charges. So for expanding your business the right way, it's just an ultimate tool.

Plus when you go there, they're also going to give you something called an IP address. That is going to be very important down the road when it comes to email marketing and search engine marketing, but I'm not going to go into too much detail about it right now. Later on I'll tell you why that's important, very important. Many hosting companies have their clients bunched under one IP address.

That's another reason to beware of cheap hosting accounts. I discovered when I was testing out different classes of hosting companies was to beware of cheap hosts because they may not stay in business. One day I woke up and started to check my sites. They were all gone. The company went under. They went under and never warned their customers. Of course, there are the obvious issues caused by their lack of customer service that you expect as well.

DEFINITION: IP ADDRESS IS A SERIES OF NUMBERS THAT IDENTIFIES YOUR LOCATION ON THE WEB AND IS USED TO VERIFY WHEN SOMEONE SUBSCRIBES OR TO FIND A SPAMMER

Now the next thing that I would do is purchase an auto-responder. Remember we were talking about building that Powerful Lead Explosion System? One of the foundation pieces is the auto-responder because it automates your communication.

You've got to build your System and your business on a solid foundation. We'll go into strategies for your auto-responder shortly and how to get started. You want to start out the right way and not allow problems later on down the road. So you get the right auto-responder. Now you might be asking yourself, what is an auto-responder? An auto-responder actually collects the names of your subscribers and clients. AND it allows you to send out emails easily and automatically. It allows you to make things happen.

Now there are two different kinds of auto-responders and you are probably aware of and thinking of what I classify as the Simple Auto-responder. The first kind of auto-responder lets you write an email that responds to emails that they system receives. Like when you are going out of town and you use the out-of-office reply feature which when someone emails you Automatically sends them back your pre-written email like "I'm out of town today, I'm going to be back next

The Ultimate Lead Generation Plan

Tuesday, so I'll talk to you then." That's the basic or Simple regular auto-responder.

The second kind is what I call a smart auto-responder and when someone sends you an email, it captures their first name, their last name, their IP address, their email address and whatever information you asked for. It also allows you to set-up forms. You can set-up forms all over the Internet and put them on different web sites. Then you begin to capture people's information — whatever information you ask for on your form. It collects all that information and allows you to segment people so you can communicate more easily and effectively.

DEFINITION: AUTO-RESPONDER IS SOFTWARE THAT ALLOWS YOU TO AUTOMATICALLY REPLY TO AN EMAIL SENT TO YOU. I.E. OUT-OF-THE-OFFICE REPLY

DEFINITION: SMART AUTO-RESPONDER IS SOFTWARE THAT ALLOWS YOU TO CREATE (ONCE AND AHEAD OF TIME) A SEQUENCE OF EMAILS DELIVERED AT A SCHEDULE DETERMINED BY YOU.

What we're going to focus on for our Lead Explosion System is the smart auto-responder. Now there are 3 different kinds of smart auto-responders. Two different kinds (Simple and Smart) and 3 different types of Smart ones. The first type is a Software Based or a Desktop Auto-responder and is actually a piece of software stored on your computer like Microsoft Word. When you buy Word, you get the disk; place it into your computer, then load the program onto your computer's hard drive. It's like Outlook on steroids. You can buy Smart versions of this desktop auto-responder.

Now the second type is what I call a Third Party Auto-responder. A third party auto-responder is a service that you pay monthly and login to access your auto-responder online. You actually logon to group website run by the company that "rents" you the access and space. We'll call it ThirdPartyAuto-responder.com and it will require you to use a user name and a password to separate you from everyone else. Once you are logged in you have access to your list, all your people, the leads that you've generated and everything is there online. So you can access your auto-responders anywhere you have a computer and an internet connection.

The third type, I call Server Based, and is actually a piece of software you purchase (similar to the first type) but you don't install it on your computer.

The Ultimate Lead Generation Plan

You have it installed onto your own hosting account. You own this software and are in complete control. Since you purchase the software there is not a monthly fee although you may want to purchase upgrades at some point in the future. Again you can access your auto-responders anywhere you have a computer and an internet connection. Now, let's look at those 3 different types that I just told you.

DEFINITION: SOFTWARE BASED AUTO-RESPONDER IS INSTALLED ON YOUR COMPUTER.

DEFINITION: THIRD PARTY AUTO-RESPONDER IS HOUSED ON A WEB SITE AND YOU SUBSCRIBE TO HAVE ACCESS TO THE SOFTWARE.

DEFINITION: SERVER BASED AUTO-RESPONDER IS INSTALLED ON YOUR OWN HOSTING ACCOUNT AND IS AVAILABLE ANYWHERE.

The first type was a piece of software that you would buy. You can order it from somebody or maybe even download it online then loaded onto your computer. Well here's the problem you may not foresee. One of my clients is Drew Miles and he helps people slash their taxes up to 60 — 70%. Some time ago Drew was out in Canada and putting on an important event and teaching with a well-known speaker. Meanwhile, Drew wanted to do this big promotion for his business. BUT he had left his computer at home, and his offer was on that computer along with all his subscribers' contact information (his list) and Software Based Auto-responder. So he was stuck! He couldn't make the promotion happen.

Just imagine how it would be for you if you were in the same situation. You go to an event or on vacation. Maybe there's a holiday coming up so you fly out to your family and to enjoy the holiday. Then all of a sudden you realize that you have a time-critical opportunity to communicate with your list but you don't have a way to do it. That's a regret-table situation, so let's scratch that first one out.

Now the second type is a third party auto-responder — read carefully on this one! A third party auto-responder is when you go to a website, you logon, you put your username, you put your password and then you can see all your auto-respon-ders. You can see your whole list; you can send out broadcasts and let people know about things like tele-seminars, your products and services and the things that keep you in business. Now here's the issue with this kind. Let's imagine that you and I and Joe Blow are all using the same auto-responder subscription service. So we are all using the same server, the same IP address, and the same system along with **lots** of other users. We all go to the same website and to get to our account. The company selling the service keeps the different accounts private and separate so no one can have access to your stuff. But everybody uses the same website off the same server. **So other users can affect you**.

DEFINITION: TELE-SEMINAR IS A PHONE-IN SEMINAR. LISTENERS CALL INTO A COMMON NUMBER (CALLED A BRIDGE LINE), TYPICALLY ENTER A PIN AND LISTEN TO A CALL. THESE CAN BE FREE OR PAID. MOST LAST 1 HOUR BUT A PAID SERIES' OF LESSONS MIGHT BE 2 HOURS EACH AND SEVERAL WEEKS IN A ROW. ALSO CALLED: TELE-CLASS, TELE-CALLS, TELE-CONFERENCES

Here is an example that I have seen played out more than once… You go to the website, login to your account and get your list. Today you are sending out an important email to your list of opt-in or double opt-in subscribers. Another user of the third party auto-responder, let's call him Joe Blow, goes out and buys 150,000 names for $50. Now that's wrong to buy a list of name first of all. If you've ever seen an opportunity like that (usually coming to you via SPAM emails), it is not really an opportunity. And if you ever see an email like that come across your screen or come across your email address, run in the opposite direction. Actually delete it, but never consider it, because you do not want to get into trouble for spamming. But in our example, as in real life, Joe Blow did not have this warning and did not use your good, ethical reasoning and he went ahead and bought that list. He sends out an email the purchased list because there is a major holiday coming up. This happens the same day that you want to send a big promotion to your opt-in for the holiday.

You are doing everything right with your list and for your promotion, but he gets his email out before you. Then you send out your emails. You and all of the other subscribers can be doing every-thing right, taking care of your lists, all developing great lists, and now sending it your emails. Now here's why Joe Blow is a **problem for you** and the other nice subscribers. Joe Blow just got in trouble with AOL and EarthLink for spamming. So these ISPs (Internet Service Providers) have to block Joe Blow from emailing/spamming their clients. So when your email comes through their server,

The Ultimate Lead Generation Plan

their filters are not checking the email address, they are filtering by IP address.

When Joe Blow sent it out his SPAM, say from Joe@JoeBlow.com his email address doesn't get in trouble, his IP address gets in trouble. Now when everyone else including you send out your emails for your big holiday promotion or for your big seminar event or your new product that you need to sell, Joe Blow has just messed it up for everyone. Your emails will not get through because EarthLink, AOL and all the other providers that just blocked Joe Blow are blocking us too because we share an IP address. Now we can't get through and there will be no promotion going out.

A specific example happened to another client and friend, Ann Preston, the founder and current President of Freedom Builders. It's a big networking organization with franchises similar to BNI (Business Network International) where people sit around a table and network together. A couple of years ago, Ann was sending emails out to let everybody know about an event. She was using a third party service and she tried to send out her email to her 5,000 subscribers and clients but only 1,000 of those emails got through. She called me up and said, "Matt, I don't know what's going on.

Nobody's responding to this offer. I have nobody coming to my seminar!" She was devastated because it was Christmas time and she was worried. She said, "I need this money. Not only for Christmas but I need it for our business because we were expecting to have this big day." It didn't happen for her right at that moment. So she asked, "Matt, what do I do?" I said, "Okay Ann, here is where we start. Let me look at what you're using."

She was using a third party auto-responder. So we got her a new hosting account to house the server based auto-responder and we moved her. It was the same software and set-up that I have been telling you about. We moved her domain name to point to her new hosting account. We installed a piece of software on her hosting account. We exported then uploaded all the people on the new auto-responder. Which is quite easy and it takes very little time to load your list over there. So now all 5,000 of her people were in the new system. She sent out another email. And she called me. She sent out the email and within 20 minutes she got over 250 emails asking 'where were you?' or responding 'we're going to come'. She calls me in tears of joy because all of a sudden, now her event is happening. It was everything that she wanted and we saved the event because of we used the third kind of auto-responder. So I just want you to think about that.

Just imagine the power of making things like that happen for you. Now the awesome part is the fact that I am teaching you how to get and use what Ann, my clients and I all use. What I recommend is a piece of software that you install on your individual hosting account because of the power you have when you install the software on your hosting account (with an individual IP address). You are in control because when you send out that email, the only person that could get you into trouble is you, nobody else.

And here's the other thing important warning about going to a third party auto-responder. They typically have a price chart that says once you get to 10,000 people then we're going to start charging you a lot more. Well, when you read and follow the strategies in this book, you will run into that "problem" of too many subscribers. Then most of them will begin charging you unbelievable amounts — every month! Instead follow my system and purchase the software once and only pay for your hosting account. And you are already paying for that! So those unnecessary expenses are the second major reason that I advise against third party auto-responders.

Now you're probably asking yourself, "What auto-responder are you talking about? What auto-responder should I get?" I'll let you know right now. It's called ARP3. You can go to <u>ARP3.com</u> or to <u>AutoResponsePlus.com</u> and view the details. When you go to the ARP3 web site you can also see what they are currently charging — last time I looked (just before publishing) it was $195 — period. At this point they are including installation (but you do the activation of the license). So you get it, you lease it from them, you install the software on your host for a year. Eventually there will be upgrades that you have the option to purchase just like when you purchase a Microsoft software product and they come out with a new version. But there is no monthly fee; you own the software license. Another reason this particular auto-responder software is great, is the tracking ability it allows you. Plus I love it because of this, when you send an email, you have another kind of control.

Pull out the highlighter... You want to control the time your subscribers receive the email so they are more likely to read the message. The **best times to send emails** are Tuesdays and Thursdays at eleven o'clock. Now if I miss Tuesday or Thursday at eleven o'clock time, I usually send my emails out

The Ultimate Lead Generation Plan

at three o'clock in the afternoon. Those are the two best times and the two best days for sending out your emails blasts based on my experience and my testing. Now, not only is that important to know but it ties closely to the kind of auto-responder you are using. When you decide you're going to send out an email at eleven o'clock or at three o'clock with ARP3, your email goes out at eleven o'clock or three o'clock. With a third party auto-responder you're in a queue, or a line, and your email goes out after the other emails that are waiting in queue are sent out.

When you have a time-sensitive email the queue will seem like days and can actually cost you several hours before your email goes through. So timing your emails to get the highest response (another aspect of control) is the third reason I recommend against third part auto-responders and for server/hosting based ARP3.

I also like AutoResponsePlus because it's IP-based just like I said before. When you send out these emails, the only person that can get you into trouble is you. Nobody else. If you were doing things wrong and you went out there and bought 150,000 names for $50, you would get shut down. But I've already warned you not to do that; so you're not going to get into trouble for that. Run your business right, treat your subscribers well and you should be perfectly fine. Plus, because you of the next strategies that you're about to study, you'll never have a problem because I'm showing you ways to get quality people.

In addition, it has tracking tags so you can communicate even more effectively with your subscribers.

Now once you buy the software you will need to have it installed. Now the first time I had it installed I spent about $500 after all was said and done. I went to Elance.com and found somebody to install it for me and it cost me… I paid the initially quoted price of $250 then they ran into problems because they didn't know what they were doing. That ended up being another fee with a total of about $500 to get installed. Now if you qualify to purchase Frontier Power Hosting, they install ARP for you plus they will activate it for you. Currently AutoResponsePlus includes installation in the price but they don't mention activation because they don't bother to do that for you.

When I started using AutoResponsePlus they didn't have installers and they certainly didn't include it in the price.

DEFINITION: SPAM THOSE UNPLEASANT EMAILS THAT YOU DID NOT ASK TO BE SENT. IF YOU ARE THE SENDER – THOSE EMAILS THAT WILL GET YOU BLOCKED BY ALL THE ISPS.

DEFINITION: ISP IS AN INTERNET SERVICE PROVIDER. COMPANIES SUCH AS AOL AND EARTHLINK THAT OFFER INTERNET ACCESS AND EMAIL ACCOUNTS.

DEFINITION: QUEUE IS TECHNO SPEAK FOR A LINE YOU WAIT IN. LIKE THE QUEUE YOU WAIT IN BEFORE YOU CAN PLACE YOUR ORDER AT A FAST FOOD PLACE.

ACTION STEPS: Immediately apply to http://FrontierPowerHosting.com to see if you qualify for their Private Hosting Account. The account includes your AutoResponsePlus license.

Chapter 5: How To Create & Control Markets

For $327 In FREE Bonuses Go To: www.PromotingTips.com/3Bonuses.htm

Chapter 6

List Building & Lead Generation Exposed

Chapter 6: List Building And Lead Generation Exposed

Now I want to show you ways to get quality people.

USING THE POWER SQUEEZE™ SITE

The next thing for you to do is to set-up your Power Squeeze™ site. You want to do set-up a Power Squeeze™ site so that you can go and powerfully squeeze the information out of people. Once that is set-up and tied to your auto-responder, we just built you a solid foundation that you can start sending massive amounts of leads to. And I'm going to tell you strategies how to get people to that site. but realize just how important and substantial this foundation that we have created is. Now we have a place for people to land. We can grab their name, we can grab their email address. And because we have the auto-responder we can market to them. Easily. We can basically get people that are hot and hungry for what we have to offer and market to them over and over and over again. And not have to worry about a thing because things are going to happen for you when you want them to.

> **ACTION STEPS**: Create your Power Squeeze™ Site on your new hosting account and tie it directly into your ARP3

Now let me give you some examples from some of my other clients. Their stories should be great motivators for you:

Drew Miles, Tax Attorney for small and start-up business owners. I mentioned him earlier; he's the one who helps you slash your taxes up to 60 to 70%. A while back he called me up and said, "Matt, I like your lifestyle." I thanked him, of course. But he said, "Here's the deal, I want to make some changes in my life." I asked what had him thinking about all this. Drew answered, "Well, I'm on the road all the time. I'm going out there and speaking at all these seminars and I want to be at home. But here's why I want to be at home, because I'm getting married pretty soon. I'm not only getting married, but I'm becoming an instant father and I want to be home with my wife and I want to spend time with my new family." He said, "I want to make this change. What do we do?"

So we met together and I asked what have you got. He showed me his website — which was a branding site with all his client resources. I said, "Oh, we need to set-up another site. I said all you've got is a branding site." He said that's what I was told that I needed. I said, "Oh no, we need to set-up a Power Squeeze™ site for you." Then I took him through the same process, everything I just showed you, and we set-up my system for Drew.

Now he does tele-seminars from home. About six (6) months after we started working together, Drew called me and he said, "Matt, thank you." And I was like thank you for what? I just replaced the income I was making out on the road. Now I can be at home and now I can choose when I want to go out. I don't have to rely on traveling to seminars to make my money. I just thought how awesome! You know it's the greatest feeling.

Not only that, his business grew so much that now he gets about 300 new subscribers a day. It used to be just him when he first started. Now it's not only just him, last count he had 8 coaches and 9 salespeople. He is happier and he grew a huge business off this system.

Chris Verhaegh, Stock and Options Course Creator and Instructor. Chris is another person that I work closely with. He had all this great information inside of him. In one year, he traded one billion dollars ($1,000,000,000) on Wall Street for the European Bank. And he was going out and teaching mutual fund managers how to trade.

Chris approached me and we started talking. He had this great information that he wanted to use to create a home study course. I said, "Well good, you start creating it but let's start working on building your list now." So he completed his home study course while his list was growing. In less than 29 days, he had over 5,000 people on his list. He did his first tele-seminar by sending out an email to promote his course. Chris made over $14,000 in one day promoting his new product.

Not only that, the week after everything continued trickling in for some time. Why? Because he had the ability to follow-up with them, he ended up doing over $36,000 on his first time coming out of the gate.

Others.   Most recently I started working with people like John Childers. I've been joint venturing with Jim Edwards on some stuff. I was just hired by a big company that's spends gobs on advertising primarily on infomercials. They hadn't even tapped the Internet but they realize that it's one of the cheapest and quickest ways to make things happen. And they came to me.

The company's called Better Trade. There's tons of new people that I've been working with. I don't know if you know Mike Litman, *Conversation with Millionaires*, I work with his team helping them start building their info-structure. He actually flew his brother, his marketing manager and his other key players to my office to see how everything works.

Chapter 7

Is It Better To Have A Big List Or A Small One?

Chapter 7: Is It Better To Have A Big List Or A Small One?

H ere's a big question a lot of people ask me. Is it better to have a big list or a small list? Does size really matter?

Now we're going to go into some strategies to make your list grow and grow the right way. But I want to give you the answer right now to "Is it better to have a big list or a small list?" To answer that, let me give you an example. At one point I had a list of 200 people and I had a list of 100,000 people (rounded but real numbers).

On the same day, I sent out the same email with the same subject line with the same offer, same everything, to the 100,000 list that I sent to the 200 list. I wanted to do a test, I wanted to see what the results would be. Now from the email blast to the

100,000 list, I ended up making about $2,000 that day. I sent out the same email to my 200 list and ended up doing $20,000 in one day. Now here's why I'm telling you this... because in this situation bigger is not better. It's not about quantity; it's about quality. You want to build a quality list. We're going to walk through the steps you can do to start building a quality list. I'll tell you, here are some of the best types of leads you can get. These are my top 5 best ways to get quality leads to start building your list.

Chapter 8

Matt's Top 5 List Building Strategies

Chapter 8: Matt's Top 5 List Building Strategies

$\mathcal{J}$ ust like my fraternity brother David Letterman, I have my own Top 5 List:

5. PRESS RELEASES

The fifth way is through Press Releases. Press Releases aren't as difficult as they once were to get in the hands of the media and more importantly your public. Now you can go to newswire services like PRweb.com where it's free to sign-up and you can send out a press release for free as well. When I'm talking about Press Releases, I'm not talking about the kind where you write it up, print it off, and mail or fax it to media outlets. I'm not talking about that old school style of Press Release because its shelf life is short, or worse they look at it and throw it in the garbage can if they don't like it. What I'm talking about is sending out your Press Releases to online newswire services. Places just like PRweb.com.

When you submit it to the newswire service, they distribute it to their contacts which include journalists, analysts, freelance writers, media outlets, newsrooms and media Web sites. In fact, PR Web emails press releases to between 60,000 and 100,000 global contacts points like these in addition to their syndication network, XML feeds and network media Web sites.

One thing you want to make sure you have on your Press Release is a link back to your Power Squeeze™ page so people can click through to sign-up for more information from you by submitting their contact information to you. Also because these Press Releases are getting archived, you'll receive a lot of back links. This is key on the FREE search side. They become archived on places like CNN and tons of other sites. They get archived so the shelf life is logged forever sometimes. These sites don't delete them, they just keep the Press Releases in their archives to be referenced. This strategy works very well in more than one aspect of the traffic game. So Press Releases are the fifth best way to build your list.

The Ultimate Lead Generation Plan

4. ADVERTISING

The fourth way is through Advertising. Basically, you can advertise in other people's newsletters. You can advertise on other people's websites. You can do advertorials. I went to Newsmax.com once. I went out and put out an advertorial and I got tons of people. You can do this too. When people clicked on the link, they went to my squeeze page and when they went to my squeeze page they signed-up and I captured their information. You can do that or you can put those small little banner ads on other's sites and have people click and go to your site and sign-up. It's just huge market, that's why it's another great way and Advertising is the fourth way to build your list.

3. SEARCH ENGINE TRAFFIC

The third way to build your list is through traffic from the search engines. There's paid traffic and there's free traffic. By paid traffic I am referring to pay for clicks or pay-per-click. When I'm talking about free traffic I'm referring to search results. For example, when you search using say Google.com. On the right-hand side of your search results there's tiny little ads that you can click on. Those are paid traffic, the advertisers pay-per-click. On the left hand side, the wider part of the page, that's free traffic.

When people click on it your link it is totally free to you and the people are sent straight to your site. When you get a lot of links coming into your site, they pull you up higher in the search engines results. So Search Engine Traffic is the third best way I have found to build your list.

2. USING ARTICLES

The second best way that I have found… and I'm so excited about this one because it's something that can go and even become viral… is through Articles. You can actually write articles. You want to write about a 300 to 700 word article. And get it out there. Submit to every place you can find on the Internet and there's locations all over the Internet that you can go and submit them to. For example EzineArticles.com is one. When you submit your information and your article to them, here is the important thing, this is a trick to highlight… Down at the bottom of your article you want to have a link back to your Power Squeeze™ page. Then when they put Your article on their website, they have to keep everything the way that you had it. Not every article gets approved but most of the time they do, as long as, and here's the thing that I learned from the first time I did it, as long as you have enough

The Ultimate Lead Generation Plan

content. You want to keep it at least 70% content and 30% can be sales. Just follow that rule of thumb and 90% of places will approve you.

Now you give it to them and they approve you and they're going to put your article on their website. Now what I have experienced and I love this, is that people will go to these websites and say yeah, I love that article. Then they'll go down to the bottom, they'll click on the link and go to your page. Not only will they do that, sometimes you'll have webmasters or people out there that are on the Internet look at these and say wow, this will be perfect for my newsletter. This will be perfect for my e-zine. This will be perfect for my website or my blog. They'll take this article and put it on their locations. And they have to keep everything the same. So your article just became viral.

Three months ago I wrote ten (10) articles and we submitted them to twenty (20) locations. After those 20 locations, I sat back and waited. At the time I think had 321 listings out there. Well last check, I have over 109,000 and I never did anything different. I just let that go and it became viral. Tons of things are happening. Google started picking things up. People started going there, taking it and putting it on their sites. And it become this huge viral thing and it keeps on growing and growing and growing month after month after month. Because more people see it, more people go get it, more people are doing the same. Not only that, the more people click on the link, more people go to your pages, and the more people that sign-up. Then naturally your list grows. So Articles are the second best way to build your list.

1. USING JOINT VENTURES

The number one, top way, to build your list is through email Joint Ventures. A Joint Venture Email is when two list owners/builders agree to introduce each other to their lists. In other words, I would send out an email talking about you and say, "Hey look, he/she's got this great newsletter or great tips and great information. Go here and sign-up for the information." And at the same time, you would send out an email to your list talking about me. That's the number one (1) best way that I've found to build your list. Here's why. It's really a massive referral. You find someone with a big list. Or the best way is when you have other list owners and group leaders that are in your industry with a list that is closely related to yours. You have them send out an email about information you have. You send out an

The Ultimate Lead Generation Plan

email in return, you can do a trade as an example. I'll send out an email to my list letting them know about you. you send an email to your list letting them know about me. Then watch what happens.

For one joint venture, we each sent out an email and in 1 day I had over 2600 people that signed-up for my list. He had about the same and it was just amazing. Overnight. Bam! It just happens. And the same thing can happen for you. I have client after client do the same thing. I created this weekly joint venture group for my clients. And they regularly do joint ventures and I get emails saying, "Wow! I ended up with 1000 new subscribers!" Or more in a day. Here's the thing, the quality is so high. That's why Joint Ventures are the first and best way that I've found to build your list.

Chapter 9

Are People Really Looking For You?

Chapter 9: Are People Really Looking For You?

So let's start getting people to your site. Don't forget what I said to you earlier: The number one best way to build your list is through Joint Ventures. But, because of the growth of the internet, there's an abundant opportunity out there. I was walking past a big screen TV in a store a while back and had to back step because of the Fox News report. They were talking about how much sales on the Internet have grown because of the large numbers of people getting on the Internet. Thus, there are an abundant number of people searching for you all the time. I don't care what business you are in. I'm using the same strategies for my businesses that I'm sharing with you right now. I've used these techniques in bricks and mortar businesses as well to target searchers in my region — many people search for the local place that has what they want to buy. But how do you know what the people are searching for?

I mentioned in the Intro that I've spent some time with 2 billionaires. The first time I walked up to the man and I asked him a question. I said, "How did you do it? How did you make it happen?" Do you know what he said to me? He said, "It was quite simple, Matt." His name is Keith Cunningham and he was actually Robert Kiyosaki's best friend at the time. Keith said this to me it's quite simple. He told me, "Here's how I did it. I went out and found out what they wanted. I went and got it and gave it to them." Now the best thing is that on the Internet, we have the power to know what people are looking for through what they are searching for.

So you can go to this location online www.GoodKeywords.com. When you look it up, just download this tool and it will tell you about the demand via the number of people out there searching for you every month. For example, one of the keywords that I'm focusing on lately is Marketing Tips. A long time ago, I said oh, it's too hard to do it, to get high up in the search engines for Marketing Tips. Because when I looked it up using the GoodKeyword, there were 60,288 people searching that phrase on Yahoo Search/Overture alone.

When you use GoodKeywords, it will tell you how many people are searching Yahoo Search/Overture on any one specific term during the previous month.

To use it after you pull up the web site, type in your keyword and press go. Then down the side of this free piece of software they'll tell you how many people are looking for that keyword. So not only did it give me marketing tips, it also gave me the number searching for Affiliate Internet Marketing Tips and other related terms.

There were another 1017 people on that one! But if you want to find out how many people are searching on a specific term in the last month all over the Internet — and if you're very optimistic — you multiply that monthly Yahoo Search/Overture number by 10. If you want to be a little conservative, like sometimes I am, you multiply it by 5. That will give you a better understanding how many people all over the Internet are searching on those specific words — words that will lead them to you.

ACTION STEPS: Look up <u>www.Good Keywords.com</u> **and download it.**

ACTION STEPS: Brainstorm some keywords for your business and begin to note the number of searches on each term you look up.

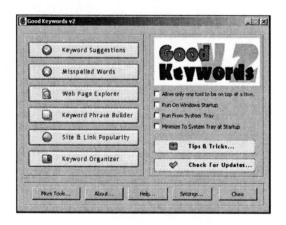

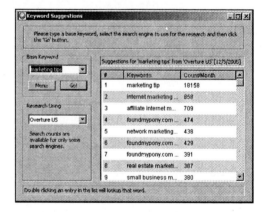

The Ultimate Lead Generation Plan

Let me give you another place to go to if you don't want to use that tool. <u>GoodKeywords.com</u> is totally free; but, if you want to pay some money to use a search tool there is another place you can go — <u>WordTracker.com</u>.

So we're focusing on getting traffic to your site. Now you know about GoodKeywords and you know how to look-up the words and terms that you think people will be using to search for you. And you have the power to go out and find how many people are searching (or not).   Then you can take those keywords and use them to pull people to your Power Squeeze™ Site. So what we really want to do is get people to you. How do we do that?

Chapter 10

Can I Buy My Way To The Top?

Chapter 10: Can I Buy My Way To The Top?

There are two different ways. There are paid ways and there are free ways. One of the paid ways to get traffic is through Pay-Per-Clicks. I'll give you some things on the free side but we can't get in depth on those in this book. I'll tell you a lot of things on the paid side. For example, there are 2 different Pay-Per-Click search engines that I personally use and recommend. The first one is called Google Adwords. The second one is called Yahoo Search (formerly Overture). There are tons of other Pay-Per-Click search engines out there. I've basically tried them all and what I discovered is most of them took a lot of my money and I never got results. Thus, I would not recommend using any others. I only recommend that you use tools that are going to make you money by giving you results.

One of the reasons I like using Pay-Per-Click services is that you can actually buy your way to become number 1, number 2, number 3. Whatever you want to be.

Back to the first one, Google Adwords. Another thing to consider is when you're using them is that they also deliver their information through EarthLink, through AOL and through Ask Jeeves. If you want to be number 1, number 2, number 3 in those locations you can make that happen with Google Adwords. NOTE: On the paid side, it is not worth it to be number 1. You want to be number 2 or number 3. We found that the highest quality people are clicking on the second and third ranking ads and more sign-up from those links on our Power Squeeze™ pages. The reason is that just anyone will see the first one and they'll click on it. They may not read your ad and you'll get a lot of junk clicks because people are like "What is that? I'll click on it." By the time they get to the second and third ad links, they're more qualified and they know that this is what they're looking for.

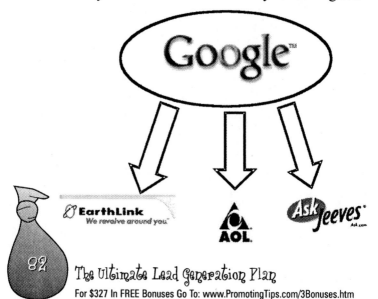

The Ultimate Lead Generation Plan
For $327 In FREE Bonuses Go To: www.PromotingTips.com/3Bonuses.htm

Now for Yahoo Search or Overture. They changed name recently since Overture is a Yahoo company. When you use them, your information is getting delivered through MSN, Alta Vista, Yahoo, Infospace and CNN. You can become number 1, number 2, number 3; wherever you want to be in there, you can buy your way to the top. Just like with Google.

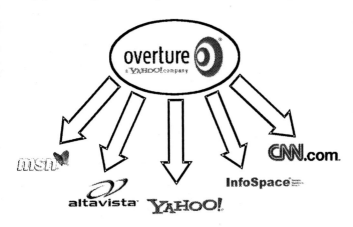

Now you might be reading this thinking, "Which one do I use? Which one do I start off with?" Well, with Google Adwords, you can actually get your account set-up and be on the Internet in less than 15 minutes. Not only, can you have your little ad sitting on the right hand side of the search results in less than 15 minutes, but people can click on it and go into your pages really quickly. Google uses software to check for your registration, keywords and ad; so the process is streamlined. Or you can go to Yahoo Search/Overture but they have people to check it so it takes a little bit longer. I had to wait about 2 weeks to get one of my accounts approved because I was using a lot of different keywords. I prefer to get up and running then add additional layers so use Google to get started while you are excited and taking action. Then add Yahoo Search to your tool belt.

A different way to decide where to start is by considering this... This is a generalization but I found this to be so true.

I play in multiple markets on the Internet always using my same system and my same strategies and one thing that my team has found and that my clients have found too is that people who use Google are more technically-minded. I'm being very general. But if you're doing something that is targeted to more technical people, you'll want to use Google or Google Adwords.

And if you are doing things that are targeted to non-technical people, we have found that Yahoo Search/Overture is the better place to go. When it comes to things in the wealth-building world, we have found that we get a lot of buyers from

The Ultimate Lead Generation Plan

Yahoo Search. In fact, we get a lot of subscribers and a lot of buyers from Yahoo Search. That's one tidbit that I wanted to share because I know it can help many of my readers.

Comparison of Yahoo Search versus Google Adwords

Yahoo/Overture Search	Google Adwords
Takes a long time to set up	Fast set-up (approximately 20 minutes)
Keywords reviewed by people (slow)	Keywords reviewed by Software (quick)
Ranking based on price paid per click	Ranking based on price and popularity (Click through rate or CTR)
Changing Ads slow	Changing Ads immediate
You can see what other sites are paying	You can't see what others are paying
Info Served at MSN, Alta Vista, Yahoo, Infospace, CNN	Info Served at EarthLink, AOL, Ask Jeeves
Attracts more non-technical people	Attracts more technical people
I use for my Wealth Building market	I use for my Promoting Tips

Chapter 11

Get Free Traffic To Your Web Site

Chapter 11: Get Free Traffic To Your Web Site

So those are paid ways to drive traffic to your sites. Not only you can do have all those paid methods but you also have the free side. Here's how I do it... when I go after a batch of new keywords, I start on the paid side. I'll jump in and start finding which keywords people are clicking on to go to my site and which keywords attract subscribers. This is possible because Auto Response Plus will allow me to track where subscribers came from, that way I'll know which keyword they used.

So I start my keyword testing on the paid side and begin collecting all my needed market data (which keywords are popular and effective for my site) and I do this for a couple of weeks. Then I can go into my list and say wow, all these people came from this specific keyword. Then I have the best direction to go in and I have an idea of what to do when I start marketing one of my websites for a specific keyword. The results take out the guesswork. Then I can effectively enter the free search engines side.

Now I can start optimizing my site for those effective keywords. I don't just do a pie-in-the-sky and just think "Oh, this one is what they're going to use to search for me." I go for what keyword produces the most subscribers. The next stage after I get that, is finding out what keyword generates the most buyers. I first optimize my site for the most subscribers, then once I get the buyers I go back to my site and optimize for the buyers. That's why right now I'm optimizing my site again.

First it was "Promoting Tips" and I ended up ranking number 1 in all the search engines on the free (organic) side for Promoting Tips. I'm number 1 on Google, I'm number 1 or close to it on MSN, Yahoo and all these places. Not only that, I just started on "Marketing Tips." One of my new clients that I have not mentioned is Tom Antion. You have probably heard of Tom. At an event we both spoke at a couple of months ago, I told him that I was making a run for Marketing Tips. He looked at me and said that he didn't know about that, that it was going to be pretty competitive. I said, "I'm going to make that happen."

The Ultimate Lead Generation Plan
For $327 In FREE Bonuses Go To: www.PromotingTips.com/3Bonuses.htm

He just attended one of my weekend workshops and I spent some time with him. During the class I said, "Tom, I'm going to show you something. Go to MSN… I'm number 4." He goes, "What, I can't believe it, that's so competitive." I said it's because these strategies work and we went over some of these strategies. If you've heard of Tom Antion, you might be asking yourself why would Tom Antion need to attend anyone's marketing class. Well here's the thing, when we were at that event I mentioned, Tom came to me and we were outside talking about some strategies. One nugget I gave him, made him say "Matt, I never even thought of that." That's when he decided to come to the workshop. He told me that he knew there were things that he didn't know and he knew that I had his answers. Sure enough, during the workshop I would see his eyes get really wide when I was covering some of my strategies.

One of the most powerful ways to optimize your site for whatever keyword that you find to be effective is through links. Each link that you have pointing to your website is like a vote. The more links you have pointing to your site, the more votes that you have, so it pulls you up higher in the search engines.

Honestly, they have a more intricate and secret process but we'll just cover the general and the biggest portion of how your Page Rank is calculated. Think about the Presidential Elections in the United States. There are a few states out there that we call swing states. There are sites on the web that have more power you can think of them as swing sites. These sites can be your California, your Florida, or your Ohio. These sites can actually help raise you higher up "in the polls" by giving you extra weighted votes if you can get a link pointing from them to your site.

So it is important to know the value of the website that you are getting a link from and the way you can find out is with a tool that you can download for free.

Go to <u>Google.com</u> and select More then select the Google toolbar or just enter this URL <u>http://toolbar.google.com/</u>. The toolbar is free. When you download the Google toolbar, it will ask if you want to **Enable advanced features** or Disable advance features. Make sure that you "**Enable** advanced features." Once you have that loaded, the toolbar appears right at the top of your browser window of your Internet program.

The Ultimate Lead Generation Plan

> **ACTION STEPS**: Download Google Toolbar at http://toolbar.google.com/ and Enable the advanced features.

As you see from the graphic (or on your screen if you jumped in and downloaded it already) in the middle of the toolbar it will have something called Page Rank. The Page Rank is the importance of the website according to Google's formula.

Websites are ranked from 0 to 10 with 10 being the highest or most important and 0 being the lowest. To increase your Page Rank you want more important sites voting/pointing toward your website. The greater the number of high ranking websites that are pointing to your site, the higher the vote count and the higher your importance which equals a higher page rank. Find your 'magic' keyword and work on getting links pointing at your site.

If you look back at some of the strategies for getting more leads coming in, you should begin to see that all of these strategies work together in some way. For example, if you send out your Press Releases, they go media outlets and are

For $327 In FREE Bonuses Go To: www.PromotingTips.com/3Bonuses.htm

archived. Not only do you have your link at the bottom of your article so that people can click and land on your Power Squeeze™ site and subscriber to your list; but you also, increased your Page Rank because those links on your articles are pointing at your website. So you concurrently are gaining subscribers while raising your Page Rank which will expose you to more potential subscribers.

Another great example is what happens with Articles. You can get your articles going all over the Internet. People will grab them and put them on their site or send your article to their list. So keep all the information the same as on Press Releases. At the bottom of the article you want to have that little bio about you and have a link that goes to your Power Squeeze™ site so people can click on it for your site. Not only that, but you are creating all these links that are pointing to your site. There's so much power that you have when creating articles. Quality strategies serve multiple purposes for growing your subscriber list.

When I'm talking about the importance of Press Releases, I'm not putting out the Releases so I can get phone calls. I'm not putting out the Press Releases so that I can get on radio shows or TV shows. I'm putting out the Press Releases, so potential subscribers will read and click on the link and land on my site. Also I want to create those links from the sites that archive the Releases and that will pull me up higher in the search engines (more votes).

When you do get that phone call or when you are asked to be on the radio to talk about your product or service or whatever it is that you offer — that's just a bonus. I had a client the other day that did her Press Releases. Two weeks later she gets a phone call and she ends up on two radio stations. She calls me up and says what do I do? I said, "Here's what I would do. When I was on the air, I would make sure to tell them about your Power Squeeze™ site. I'd say go to this site.com. Mention your site so listeners can subscribe." You can get this kind of visibility from just one of the strategies that I have covered.

Once you start implementing these strategies, they start building-up momentum and more things keep on happening. As your list grows, so does your bank account. I've noticed as my list grows, I look at my bank account and the bank account goes along with it. Sometimes my bank account goes higher than my list because the longer you have a list, the more relationships you build through the emails that your auto-responders are automatically sending out. I have one auto-responder that I set-up with 2 years worth of information going out to the subscribers. That's two years of communications from me. I also have short emails that go out and ask people click on links which takes them to a sales letter page to buy stuff from me. We have over 750 to 1000 people subscribing every day just on one of my lists. That's just huge. That's the huge kind of kind you can create for yourself using the strategies I have covered in this book. It's so powerful.

Chapter 12

Don't Get It
Right, Get It
Going

Chapter 12: Don't Get It Right, Get It Going

There's a question that everybody always asks me. "Matt, when do I start building my list? When do I start?" Well let me tell you, **start now!** Don't wait, I don't care where your product is, I don't care where your service is, I don't care if you're still working on getting it all together. Start building your list now. That means you build more relationships and stronger relationships. Just imagine if you have a product that you're working on or a seminar that you're creating or even if you're thinking about doing a seminar a year from now. You know in your mind that you're going to do it. Start building that list now so you have relationships built and a number of quality people on your list. Then when ready to launch, you will see bigger results than if you don't build a system now and instead wait until the last minute.

It's just like when my office was broken into a while back. Somebody broke in then I went out and bought a security alarm. That's a very similar approach to waiting until your product is sitting on your shelf before building your prospect database. You can be building your list right now.

I swear this is one of the most important, biggest things that I want you to understand and act on. **Start building your list now** — do not wait. You want to do it right now.

Closing Ideas And Magical Thoughts...

TEST, TEST, TEST...

Testing is essential to your results. We test things like: Where to place things on a site, what colors work best, what words work best, and we always test headlines.

ACT AND GROW RICH

I want to ask you another question. Have you ever come up with an idea and hesitated? Then found out that somebody had the idea too and they ran with it. Now because you didn't take advantage of an opportunity that you saw, they have your market share. This actually goes for me too. I watch one of two things. I watch either movies or I watch infomercials. Those are my two favorite things to watch because I get a lot of these great ideas. One day I was watching CBC or the Home Shopping Network, I was just listening to the people and seeing what they do. One product I saw, I thought Man I knew that. Oh gosh, I thought of that years ago. And here is this person making millions of dollars off this idea. Here's the lesson: I hesitated. I didn't make things happen then — please don't put yourself in that same situation.

THE FTC SUCKS

Now let me tell you about this too. You might have heard this story. There is somebody out there that experienced getting their website shut down. They were doing millions of dollars on the Internet. Their website got shut down by the FTC. You want to know why? Here's why: Because they didn't know what they didn't know. My question to you right now is this, **what is it that you don't know that you don't know?** And I truly want you to take a minute and think about that.

TWO COMMON CHARACTERISTICS OF HIGHLY SUCCESSFUL PEOPLE

1. **Highly Successful People are <u>ACTION-ORIENTED</u>**. This means they take action <u>immediately</u> when a good opportunity presents itself.

The Ultimate Lead Generation Plan

2. **Highly Successful People are <u>EDUCATION-FOCUSED</u>**. This means that they take it upon themselves to know everything they possibly can about their field, and they learn from many different sources.

Are you Action-Oriented? Are you Education-Focused? Are you a Highly Successful Person?

YOU ARE RIPPING ME OFF

One last thing is this and I'm going to be very serious. I'm about to tell you something I went through. I built a multi-million dollar business after being totally bankrupt, I mean I had nothing. The remarkable thing is I changed something in my mind and it was because of this that I realized something life-altering. Now, I want to pass this long to you. This was the turning point for thing starting to take off for me. You see, I realized that I was ripping you off…

I had all this magical, powerful information inside my head. I had all this information and this expertise that I could share with people and I didn't. Let me say it this way so you can relate. You are ripping people off. If you do not go out there and market to people and let people know about your information, then you are ripping people off. Because it's your job, it's your right and it's your responsibility to go out there and to let people know about the information, about the products and about the services that you have to offer. Because if you don't, if you do not go out there and start marketing, persuading and letting people know about that information, about your products and about your services… then you're not only ripping me off but you're ripping off the world. And do you know what else? You're not only ripping off the world but you're ripping yourself off. You could be putting a lot of money in your back pocket that you're not.

It is your responsibility to go out there and do this. Think of the lives that you can change. And the lives that you can change, can impact so many more. And not only that, but you can impact your family. Nothing's worse, I remember when I was going through those troubled times and I was looking in my wife's eyes and I was looking my family's eyes and I knew I couldn't give them things. I remember there was a time I couldn't give my family Christmas presents. But now it's like I'm going to buy tons of things for my family.

Remember I'm buying a restaurant because my dad works in China. He can't come home because

The Ultimate Lead Generation Plan

he's kind of stuck to his job. And I'm doing that so I can replace my dad's income and he can come home and be with the family and just saying there's purpose for everything.

Now I have the ability because I know I've been going out there and I've been helping so many people. The more people you help, the more people you go out there and you have that continuing education. The more that you will benefit too and so will they. It just helps everybody. It's your responsibility to do that. I want to tell you that it has been an honor and a privilege to write this book to share with you and to teach you. It's my responsibility to tell you this information. I want to make sure that you have it so you can grow and some things can happen for you. I want to see you successful, because I understand you. I have been in your shoes.

Contacting The Author

Matt Bacak, "The Powerful Promoter" is not only a sought-after Internet Marketer but also has marketed for some of the world's top experts whose reputations would shrivel if their followers ever found out someone else coached them on their online marketing strategies.

Matt, an entrepreneur from the time he could pull a wagon, started his first company with employees at the age of 12. He hasn't slowed down since! And now he helps others benefit from his experience and gifts through his consultations, coaching, and workshop programs.

Matt has a unique ability to take a vast amount of complex information — often conflicting — and boil it down to the core essence of what works, the easiest path, and he makes it simple all at the same time.

Matt Bacak welcomes your communications. He is available, schedule permitting, for speaking and seminar engagements, consulting, and marketing assignments. To contact Matt Bacak concerning any of these or similar matters, it is best to call his office or visit his website at:

www.PowerfulPromoter.com

To contact Matt Bacak's office:
Office number is 1-770-271-1536
Fax number is 1-770-234-5389

108

The Ultimate Lead Generation Plan
For $327 In FREE Bonuses Go To: www.PromotingTips.com/3Bonuses.htm

Claim Your 3 FREE Bonuses Now

$327 VALUE
FREE BONUSES

On the following pages, you will find three valuable bonuses that are guaranteed to help you EXPLODE your business.

The first is a consultation where you will participate in a telephone interview. Matt wants YOU to be the next overnight success story of his Internet Millionaire Intensive! Matt needs your success story this year and wants to teach you the secrets of success for earning millions of dollars in information marketing. *(A $200 Value) –See the next page!*

The second is a subscription to Matt Bacak's Promoting Tips Newsletter. You'll learn 'secrets' that most people will never know about how to really explode their online newsletter, ezine or e-course opt-ins in no time flat. If you have an email account, then you can discover the most powerful strategies to volcanically erupt your online newsletter opt in subscriber databases while making more cold hard cash. *(A $100 Value)*

The third is Matt Bacak's Best selling CD "The Lead Explosion System – How To Automatically Generate Fanatical Buyers." *(A $27 Value)*

Certain Restrictions do apply, as stated on the following pages.

TO CLAIM ALL 3 BONUSES VALUED AT $327 SIMPLY GO TO:

www.PromotingTips.com/3Bonuses.htm

FREE "Internet Millionaire" Consultation

Matt Bacak is showing an elite, hand-picked group of people just like you how to...Create MASSIVE Wealth using the Power of the Internet!

...WILL YOU BE NEXT?

The Ultimate Lead Generation Plan

For $327 In FREE Bonuses Go To: www.PromotingTips.com/3Bonuses.htm

"Just *read this book* then fill out the form below to **officially apply** to become a member of my exclusive *'Internet Millionaire Intensive,'* where I'll show an elite hand-picked group of my best students how to...Create <u>MASSIVE Wealth</u> using the Internet!"

If you qualify, we will advance you to stage #2 of the application process, where you will participate in a private telephone interview. Matt wants YOU to be the next overnight success story of his *Internet Millionaire Intensive*!

This is your chance at having **Matt Bacak, The Powerful Promoter**, help you explode your business so you can gain personal and financial FREEDOM. Matt Bacak's proven secrets and techniques have turned 100's of businesses into overnight success stories and now they are touching the lives of HUNDREDS OF THOUSANDS of people worldwide!

☑ Yes, Matt! I WANT to apply to become a member of your exclusive "Internet Millionaire Intensive! Please sign me up for private telephone interview with one of your personally trained specialists.

Name:_____

Email address:_____

Telephone number:_____

Best times EST. to call:_____

Call Toll Free 1-866-MATT-123
Or Mail To: The Powerful Promoter,
2935 Horizon Park Drive, Suite D, Suwanee, GA 30024
Or You Can Fax to 770-234-5389

Glossary

Auto-responder — is software that allows you to Automatically reply to an email sent to you. I.E. Out-of-the-Office Reply

Blog — is a form of communication written from a personal perspective for public consumption like a online diary.

Branding Site — allows prospects to learn about you and your business

Domain — is a web address or a URL.

Hard Drive Space — is where you store all of your hosting files such as the web sites you create

IP Address — is a series of numbers that identifies your location on the web and is used to Verify when someone subscribes or to Find a Spammer

ISP — is an Internet Service Provider. Companies such as AOL and Earthlink that offer internet access and email accounts.

Joint Ventures — It's a kind of like a partnership, where people send out emails to help each other out and/ or make money.

Organic Search — is "free" search engine traffic

Power Squeeze™ Site — captures the contact information of your prospects.

Sales Letter Site — sells a product, service or event

Server Based Auto-responder — is installed on your own hosting account and is available anywhere.

Smart Auto-responder — is software that allows you to create (once and Ahead of time) a sequence of emails delivered at a schedule determined by you.

Software Based Auto-responder — is installed on your computer.

SPAM — those unpleasant emails that you did not ask to be sent. If you are the sender — Those emails that will get you blocked by all the ISPs.

Subdomain — is like a mini-site on your hosting account and can be pointed to different folders in your web space, for example http://subdomain.mymaindomain.com.

The Ultimate Lead Generation Plan

Tele-seminar — is a phone-in seminar. Listeners call into a common number (called a Bridge line), typically enter a PIN and listen to a call. These can be free or paid. Most last 1 hour but a paid series' of lessons might be 2 hours each and several weeks in a row. Also called: Tele-class, Tele-calls, Tele-conferences.

Third Party Auto-responder — is housed on a web site and you subscribe to have access to the software.

Queue — is techno speak for a line you wait in. Like the Queue you wait in before you can place your order at a fast food place.

Checklist

❏ Go to www.FrontierPowerHosting.com:

▦ Complete Application process and instructions will follow

▦ Move your domain name server (DNS) if necessary...

❏ Go to your new domain — the root directory is already up if you purchased from www.FrontierPowerHosting.com

❏ Create your Power Squeeze™ Page and tie the form directly into your new ARP software

❏ Look up www.GoodKeywords.com and download it.

❏ Brainstorm some keywords for your business and begin to note the number of searches on each term you look up.

❏ Download the Google Toolbar at http://toolbar.google.com/ and Enable the advanced features.

Printed in the United States
41687LVS00001B/301-411